Inside the NBA

New York Knicks

Paul Joseph

ABDO & Daughters
PUBLISHING

Published by Abdo & Daughters, 4940 Viking Dr., Suite 622, Edina, MN 55435.

Copyright ©1997 by Abdo Consulting Group, Inc., Pentagon Tower, P.O. Box 36036, Minneapolis, Minnesota 55435. International copyrights reserved in all countries. No part of this book may be reproduced in any form without written permission from the publisher. Printed in the United States.

Cover photo: Duomo
Interior photos: Allsport, pages 5, 21, 23, 26
Wide World Photos, pages 1, 7, 9, 11, 12, 17, 22, 25

Edited by Ken Berg

Library of Congress Cataloging–in–Publication Data

Joseph, Paul, 1970-
    The New York Knicks / by Paul Joseph.
        p. cm. — (Inside the NBA)
    Includes index.
    Summary: Discusses some of the key players and coaches and important games in the up-and-down history of the New York Knicks.
    ISBN 1-56239-767-2 $16.48
    1. New York Knickerbockers (Basketball team)—History—Juvenile literature. [1. New York Knickerbockers (Basketball team)—History. 2. Basketball—History.] I. Title. II. Series.
GV885.52.N4J67   1997
796.323' 64' 097471—dc21   96-39607
                                                                                CIP
                                                                                AC

Contents

New York Knicks

No city lives, breathes, and dies basketball more than New York. Fans follow hundreds of high school and college teams throughout the Big Apple. But when the NBA's (National Basketball Association) Knicks are in town and playing well, everybody else takes a back seat in New York City.

From their days as a small, quick, scrappy, and defensive unit under Joe Lapchick, to the championship years between 1969 and 1973, to Pat Riley's physical squads led by Patrick Ewing, to the present team led by young, solid players, the Knicks have always played a never-say-die style of basketball that New Yorkers have come to love.

Although the Knicks have had their share of disappointing seasons and can claim only two NBA titles in their long history, few other events have that certain electricity of a Knick's game in Madison Square Garden.

The fact is, most of the Knicks teams have ranged from mediocre to bad, but the fans still talk about the championship years. They will compare today's teams to the championship squads of 1970 and 1973. Which, in truth, rank among the best ever in the history of the NBA.

Facing page: The Knicks' Patrick Ewing.

The Knicks of the 1970s had every corner covered. There was Willis Reed's stamina and determination, Clyde Frazier's clutch play, Bill Bradley's unbelievable court sense, Earl Monroe's incredible skills, and Dave DeBusschere's toughness. Those players combined to make one of the best teams ever, and give the New York fans excitement year in and year out.

After the 1970s the Knicks slipped into mediocrity. But when Patrick Ewing was drafted No. 1 in 1984, the Knicks began a new era with Ewing eventually leading them to the Eastern Finals.

Although Ewing provides the leadership, the Knicks have added some young stars. The 1996 draft was considered the best ever for New York, not to mention one of the best ever in the NBA. The Knicks grabbed three premium players—John Wallace of Syracuse, Walter McCarty of Kentucky, and Dontae Jones of Mississippi State—who will certainly get the New York fans excited again and fill the seats at the Garden.

Max Zaslofsky is fouled as he attempts a pass.

The Early Years

Before and immediately after World War II, basketball was principally a high school and college sport. Ned Irish ran the college program in New York, highlighted by games at Madison Square Garden.

Irish decided he would like to try his luck with a professional team. Salaried basketball had not yet caught on and Irish was therefore taking a chance. Yet he was confident that New Yorkers would fill the Garden to see his New York Knicks play in the new Basketball Association of America (BAA).

On November 1, 1946, the Knicks opened in Toronto against the Huskies. A crowd of 7,090 watched the Knicks win an exciting, typically low-scoring, 68-66 game. But back in New York, no one paid attention; fans still preferred the college game.

Irish nevertheless believed in the Knicks. In 1947, he hired Joe
Lapchick, the legendary coach of St. John's University. Irish
correctly judged that getting him would draw more local interest to
the Knicks.

Led by Sid Tannenbaum and Carl Braun, the Knicks made it to
the BAA playoffs in 1947, but were eliminated in the first round. In
1948, the BAA and the National Basketball League (NBL) merged to
form the NBA.

Even with the merger, the NBA was still a tough sell. Teams
folded, others joined, and others folded again. But the Knicks
remained intact. Behind Lapchick's reputation and excellent
coaching, the Knicks began to fill the Garden and play solid ball.

By 1951, the Knicks were in the NBA Finals fighting it out for
the championship. Lapchick's solid, deep unit with no superstars
learned how to win.

Max Zaslofsky led the Knicks with a 14.1 points per game
average. Dick McGuire was the point guard and could really dish the
ball, setting a team record with 17 assists against the Milwaukee
Hawks. Vince Boryla was the clutch forward. Harry Gallatin, Connie
Simmons, Ernie Vandeweghe, and Nat Clifton rounded out the
lineup.

This young squad had surprised the Boston Celtics and Syracuse
Nationals in the playoffs. But in the championship the Knicks were
down three games to none in the best-of-seven against the Rochester
Royals. With the series all but over, the Knicks fought back to pick
up three close victories.

The series was now tied, and the Knicks had a chance at their
first title. Game 7 was deadlocked 75-75 with under a minute left,
before Rochester pulled it out 79-75. New York lost the
championship, but the "no-name Knicks," with their furious
comeback and scrappy play, won the hearts of once-skeptical fans.
Now the Knicks were truly "New York's team."

Three-In-A-Row

The 1952 season found the Knicks continuing with their winning habits. At season's end New York had to settle for third place, but still good enough for the playoffs. In the playoffs the Knicks played smarter, scrappier, and with more determination, and won the East again by eliminating the Celtics and Nationals.

In the Finals, the Knicks were matched against the NBA's first dynasty, the Minneapolis Lakers. The Knicks fought all the way to the seventh game, but lost the series.

Point guard
Dick McGuire

The turning point actually happened in the first game. With only seconds left in overtime, McGuire drove to the hoop and was fouled. The foul was called, but both referees missed seeing the ball go in the basket! Everyone else at the game saw the shot go in— except the two refs. The Lakers won the game, and the remainder of the seven-game series was split.

In 1953, the Knicks posted a 47-23 regular season record, cruising through the playoffs with wins over the Baltimore Bullets and Boston, to capture their third straight Eastern Conference title.

The Knicks finally believed they had the team to be the NBA champions. And they proved it in Game 1, winning in dramatic fashion 96-88. Yet that was all the Knicks could muster against the always tough Lakers. Minneapolis dominated every facet of the next four games.

The Knicks had been to the Finals three years in-a-row, but couldn't get the job done. It would be 17 more years before they got that close. One thing was for sure in the those early years: the Knicks played hard and won games with less talent than most teams. Foremost, they gained respect in a city where respect doesn't come easy.

Cazzie Russell shows off his ball-handling style.

The Long Descent

The Knicks boasted the best team in the East again in 1954, but in the playoffs they were ousted by the Celtics. The Knicks again were eliminated in 1955 by the Celtics, and this time they never really recovered.

Midway through the 1956 season, Joe Lapchick began to feel the pressure of coaching in the toughest sports town in the country and announced his retirement. Vince Boryla took over, but couldn't turn the squad around. The Knicks sat out the playoffs for the first time in the team's history. It was the start of a decade of losing.

Between 1957 and 1967, the Knicks finished in last place nine times. Bad coaching and horrible draft selections, such as taking Kenny Sears over Bill Russell and Paul Hogue instead of John Havlicek or Chet Walker, were some of the reasons for the Knicks' poor performances.

In 1959, the team turned the corner and made it to the playoffs, but were eliminated in the first round. The Knicks fell right back into the cellar.

It wasn't until the mid-60s that the Knicks began to build for the future. The team wasn't winning many games, but one could sense the talent forming.

Willis Reed, Cazzie Russell, Walt Frazier, Phil Jackson, Dick Barnett, and Bill Bradley were the Knicks' future. But in their early years it was difficult for coaches to discipline and bring these young players together. Substitute Freddie Crawford even fell asleep once on the bench during a game!

Then, in December 1967, Red Holzman took over as head coach and began to shape things up. In Holzman's first year, the team made it to the playoffs. Although the Knicks were ousted in the opening round, they knew it was only a matter of time before this budding team would be champions.

Walt Frazier slides by 76ers' defenders as he heads for an easy layup.

Knicks' First Championship

The Knicks added one more solid player to their talented lineup in the 1968-69 season, trading for Dave DeBusschere. It looked as though the makings for a championship team were now in place.

The Knicks felt they could win the East in 1969. And they did. Then they swept the Bullets four straight in the first-round of the playoffs. Then they ran into the Celtics; the Celtics won the series four games to two and went on to take the NBA's top honors.

It was not meant to be for the Knicks that year. But everyone knew that with a lineup like the one they had, they would certainly be back.

The Knicks were the favorite going into 1969-70, but few anticipated how they would dominate to the degree they did. The Knicks started 23-2 and the rest of the league might as well have quit then. The Knicks were close to unbeatable.

There were no individual stars on this talented group. Their balanced attack featured a pressing defense and an intelligent offense that moved the ball and scored with high-percentage shots.

New York fans couldn't get enough of this edition of the Knicks. Getting a ticket to a game was next to impossible—it was easily the best show in town.

The Knicks ran through the regular season with 60 wins. But there was a scare in the first round of the playoffs, as they narrowly escaped the Washington Bullets four games to three.

In the Eastern Finals, the Knicks got back on track, beating the Milwaukee Bucks four games to one. After 17 years, the Knicks found themselves back in the NBA Finals. Their opponent was the equally talented Los Angeles Lakers, featuring Wilt Chamberlain, Elgin Baylor, and Jerry West.

Game 1 was all Willis Reed. He scored 37 points and hauled in 16 rebounds while holding his counterpart Chamberlain to 17 points. The Knicks won 124-112. Game 2 was much closer, as the Lakers edged the Knicks 105-103 to tie the series.

The next two games went into overtime with each team grabbing a victory. The Knicks won the fifth game, 107-100, but the bad news was the injury to Willis Reed. Reed tore his right thigh muscle and was said to be out for the rest of the series.

Without Reed, Chamberlain dominated Game 6 with 45 points and 27 rebounds. The Lakers stomped all over the Knicks with the biggest margin of the series, 135-113. The Lakers were confident and ready to "win it all" in Game 7.

Madison Square Garden was unusually quiet for the start of the biggest showdown in Knick's history. Then the crowd roared when the announcer introduced Willis Reed as a surprise starter at center.

Reed was barely able to walk, let alone run, but was determined to stop Chamberlain and the Lakers. The Knicks darted to an early lead and never looked back, winning 113-99. The New York Knicks had their first championship.

Willis Reed's unprecedented courage and dominating play earned him places on the All-Defensive Team and the All-NBA Team. He also was the Final's Most Valuable Player (MVP), the All-Star Game's MVP, and the league's overall MVP. No Knick player has ever matched Reed's incredible season.

More Championship Seasons

After the NBA championship season, there was quite a letdown. In 1970-71 the Knicks coasted during the regular season, winning 52 games behind their tough defense. Walt Frazier led the offense with 21 points per game.

In the playoffs, the Knicks manhandled the Hawks four games to one. But the second round would be too much for New York. The Baltimore Bullets, led by Wes Unseld and Earl Monroe, knocked off the defending champs in a seven-game battle.

The following year, the Knicks added two players to strengthen an already solid roster. Jerry Lucas was acquired from the Golden State Warriors to back up Willis Reed, who was ailing from bad knees. And there was a trade for one of the best guards at that time— Earl "the Pearl" Monroe.

Lucas filled in well for Reed, averaging 16 points and 12 rebounds per game. Monroe, on the other hand, had trouble tuning into the Knicks' system, which sacrificed high individual numbers for teamplay. But Monroe wanted a championship, so he worked to integrate himself into a proven system.

The Knicks put it all together and won the Eastern Finals, then headed into the NBA Finals. They were matched against the Lakers in what was touted as a great match-up, even though the Knicks had to deal with injuries. After winning the opener, the Knicks were dispatched in four straight.

New York came back even more determined the following year. The 1973 Knicks won with a combination of unselfish offense, intense defense, and determination. Monroe became the offensive sparkplug, while Reed and Lucas combined to average 20 points per game. Again, like the champs of 1970, no one player shined. The Knicks won on the strength of team play and—still again—their league-leading defense.

The Knicks ran by the Bullets in the first round of the playoffs, four games to one. In the Eastern championship, the Knicks and Celtics battled for seven games. In the closing game at the Boston Garden, with the momentum with the Celtics, the Knicks came out and dominated with tenacious defense, winning 94-78.

In the NBA Finals, New York met fierce rival, Los Angeles. This would be the third Finals between them in four years, each having won once.

The Lakers, still led by Chamberlain and West, edged the Knicks in Game 1, 115-112. After that, however, it was all New York. The Knicks put their defense in high gear and clamped down on the Lakers. Los Angeles never reached the century mark again. The Knicks cruised through the four following games to bring their second championship back to New York.

The Knicks featured outstanding all-around team ball, led by Willis Reed, who was named Finals MVP. The Knicks proved to everyone that team defense and team play, as opposed to offensive stars, can win championships. The Knicks championship teams of the early 70s were among the very best to ever play in the NBA.

Willis Reed.

Two-Decade Drought

The Knicks team had grown older, and injuries began to bring them down in 1973-74. They did make the playoffs, but were run over by the Celtics in five games in the second round.

After the season, Willis Reed, Jerry Lucas, and Dave DeBusschere retired. Ned Irish, founder of the Knicks, stepped down as president of the club. The 1975 Knicks played less than .500 ball, but did slip into the playoffs. They were, however, ousted in the first round.

The Knicks continued to add solid players to the lineup, acquiring Spencer Haywood, Bob McAdoo, and Jim McMillan in hopes of rebuilding a winner. Although these additions helped, the retirement of Bill Bradley hurt more. Another sub-.500 season left the Knicks in need of more change—including management.

New York

Max Zaslofsky led the Knicks in 1951 with a 14.1-points-per-game average.

Point guard Dick McGuire set a team record in a 1951 game with 17 assists.

Willis Reed was named Finals MVP for his outstanding play in the 1973 NBA Finals.

Knicks

Patrick Ewing won the Rookie of the Year Award for his 1985-86 debut performance with the Knicks.

Power forward Charles Oakley was acquired by the Knicks in 1988.

John Starks helped the Knicks capture the 1993-94 Eastern Conference Championship.

Willis Reed became the Knicks' new coach. He would lead them to a 43-39 record and a first-round victory in the playoffs, but that was it. The following season, Reed was fired after only 14 games.

In 1979, the Knicks chose Michael Ray Richardson in the first round of the draft. Although it was a good pick and he proved to be a solid player, they could have chosen Larry Bird, who was still available. The young team had some promising players in Richardson, Bill Cartwright, and Ray Williams, but they finished out of the playoffs at 39-43.

By 1982, the team was in last place and players were being traded or leaving via free-agency. Hubie Brown became head coach in 1983 and brought in a slow, deliberate style of offense that was to revolve around Bernard King. King was the Knicks' new scoring machine acquired from Golden State in return for Richardson.

Behind King, Cartwright, and Brown's new offensive scheme, the Knicks were back above .500. In the playoffs, New York won in the first round, but was manhandled in the second round by the Philadelphia 76ers.

In 1983-84, Bernard King became a legitimate star in the NBA. He led the Knicks to the playoffs and in scoring. King's finest performance took place in the first round of the playoffs, scoring 40 or more points in 4 straight games and virtually beating the Detroit Pistons by himself.

In the second round, the Knicks stretched the Celtics to seven games, but Boston prevailed. The Knicks' chance of going back to the Finals was over.

In 1984-85, injuries dropped the Knicks from a power to one of the least productive teams in the league. The Knicks won only 24 times, but New Yorkers were somewhat comforted because they would get the No. 1 pick in the following year's draft.

The Knicks Get Ewing

In 1985, the New York Knicks chose the most sought after college player in Patrick Ewing. A seven-foot, one-inch center, Ewing was the man the Knicks looked to for rebuilding the franchise.

Ewing promptly garnered the Rookie of the Year Award, while the Knicks finished as the NBA's best defensive team. But offensively, they were last, thanks mainly to the fact that King was out all season and Cartwright played in only two games.

In 1986, the Knicks were just as unsuccessful. They released King and fired Hubie Brown, winning only 24 games in a season many thought hopeless.

Patrick Ewing fights for two points under the basket.

Then Rick Pitino was hired as coach. Pitino had young players like Ewing, Marc Jackson, Gerald Wilkins, and Kenny Walker, who all possessed speed, enthusiasm, and endurance. So Pitino instituted a running game that utilized a full-court press. The game was fun again and the Knicks were coming around.

By 1988-89, the Knicks were again playing winning ball under the new system. Cartwright was traded for Charles Oakley, a natural power forward. Rod Strickland, another talented guard, came in the draft.

The Knicks won 52 games and swept the 76ers in the first round of the playoffs. But many thought this young team was too cocky and overconfident going into the next series. It showed, as they were drubbed by the Bulls in six games.

Still, most New York fans loved the new style and were getting ready for the 1989-90 season—hopefully a championship one. But it

wasn't to be. Rick Pitino left New York to coach the University of Kentucky Wildcats, and Stu Jackson took over.

Jackson couldn't get the team in gear and was fired halfway through the 1990-91 campaign. John MacLeod assumed control but the team failed to respond. The front-office knew something had to be done.

Left: Charles Oakley blocks out Orlando Magic guard Brian Shaw.

Knicks' head coach
Pat Riley.

Pat Riley Comes To The Big-Apple

The Knicks cleaned house in 1991-92. Pat Riley, who had led the Los Angeles Lakers to several championships in the 1980s, became head coach. Riley stressed defense—the same type of defense the Knicks had played decades before.

Ewing, Oakley, Jackson, Xavier McDaniel, Anthony Mason, and John Starks played hard, consistent, physical basketball that got them back into playoff form.

In the first round, the Knicks squeaked past the Pistons. In the second round they met the defending world champion Chicago Bulls, led by superstar Michael Jordan. It was a bruising, sometimes angry seven-game battle. Although the Bulls prevailed, it was obvious the Knicks had a winning combination.

The 1992-93 Knicks stomped through the regular season with a belligerent, sometimes even roughhouse, tactic designed to knock off the Bulls. Ewing had another tremendous season, as did others on the roster. But in the playoffs, the Knicks were not able to wrestle the crown away from the talented Bulls.

Back To The Finals

The 1993-94 Knicks got a break with the surprise retirement of Chicago's Michael Jordan. The Knicks were therefore proclaimed the team to beat in the East and possibly the entire NBA.

New York sailed through the regular season and the playoffs, winning the Eastern Conference championship. The Knicks had finally made it back to the Finals after more than two decades!

The Knicks were trying for their third NBA title. Confronting Hakeem Olajuwon and the Houston Rockets was no easy task, but the Knicks were the favorites going in.

The series went back and fourth, coming down to a seventh and deciding game. But it wasn't to be for the Knicks. The Rockets prevailed and Olajuwon—not Ewing—was named the MVP of the series.

Most NBA observers predicted the Knicks and Rockets would meet again the following year. Both teams were stacked with talent and everybody wanted to see another rematch between Ewing and Olajuwon.

The Rockets made it back, but the Knicks were upset in the playoffs by the Indiana Pacers. Olajuwon and the Rockets took another title while the dejected Knicks watched from their living rooms.

Many changes took place in the Knicks organization in 1995-96— a new coach and new players. But the biggest change didn't involve the Knicks at all—Michael Jordan was back in Chicago for his first full season since his short-lived fling with professional baseball.

And, again, the Knicks couldn't get past the talented Bulls—as they were trounced in five games.

John Starks drives past an Atlanta Hawks defender on his way to the basket.

A Bright Future And A Historic Past

The Knicks came out in the 1996-97 season with the leadership and awesome play of Patrick Ewing, who guaranteed an NBA championship for the Knicks. But the bigger news was Ewing's fresh teammates. The Knicks acquired stars Larry Johnson, Allan Houston, and Chris Childs—all quality players for their former teams.

They also had the best draft in the Knicks' history, picking John Wallace, Walter McCarty, and Dontae Jones. All three of the young talented players will make a huge impact in the future.

The Knicks won 10 more games than the year before, posting a 57-25 record in 1996-97. In the postseason the Knicks trounced the Charlotte Hornets in the first round. In the second round New York came out and started doing the same to the Miami Heat. They were up three games to one and looked like a championship team. Then disaster struck.

Facing page: The Knicks' Larry Johnson gets set to pass the ball off.

In Game 5, P.J. Brown of the Heat flipped Knicks' guard Charlie Ward out of bounds and a fight began between the two. Many New York players left the bench, which is an automatic one-game suspension. The suspended Knicks' players included Patrick Ewing and John Starks. From that point on it was never the same for New York. Miami won three games in a row to steal the series and send the talented Knicks home. Patrick Ewing's guarantee of a NBA championship didn't come true.

It was a horrible way to end such a fine season. The experts, however, will continue to watch the Knicks. Many believe that with a talented young cast led by the veteran All-Star Patrick Ewing, the Knicks should eventually get that NBA title. But even if they don't, fans can still talk about the great New York Knicks' teams of the late 1960s and early 1970s.

Glossary

American Basketball Association (ABA)—A professional basketball league that rivaled the NBA from 1967 to 1976 until it merged with the NBA.

assist—A pass of the ball to the teammate scoring a field goal.

Basketball Association of America (BAA)—A professional basketball league that merged with the NBL to form the NBA.

center—A player who holds the middle position on the court.

championship—The final basketball game or series, to determine the best team.

draft—An event held where NBA teams choose amateur players to be on their team.

expansion team—A newly-formed team that joins an already established league.

fast break—A play that develops quickly down court after a defensive rebound.

field goal—When a player scores two or three points with one shot.

Finals—The championship series of the NBA playoffs.

forward—A player who is part of the front line of offense and defense.

franchise—A team that belongs to an organized league.

free throw—A privilege given a player to score one point by an unhindered throw for goal from within the free-throw circle and behind the free-throw line.

guard—Either of two players who initiate plays from the center of the court.

jump ball—To put the ball in play in the center restraining circle with a jump between two opponents at the beginning of the game, each extra period, or when two opposing players each have control of the ball.

Most Valuable Player (MVP) Award—An award given to the best player in the league, All-Star Game, or NBA Finals.

National Basketball Association (NBA)—A professional basketball league in the United States and Canada, consisting of the Eastern and Western conferences.

National Basketball League (NBL)—A professional basketball league that merged with the BAA to form the NBA.

National Collegiate Athletic Association (NCAA)—The ruling body which oversees all athletic competition at the college level.

personal foul—A player foul which involves contact with an opponent while the ball is alive or after the ball is in the possession of a player for a throw-in.

playoffs—Games played by the best teams after the regular season to determine a champion.

postseason—All the games after the regular season ends; the playoffs.

rebound—To grab and control the ball after a missed shot.

rookie—A first-year player.

Rookie of the Year Award—An award given to the best first-year player in the league.

Sixth Man Award—An award given yearly by the NBA to the best non-starting player.

trade—To exchange a player or players with another team.

Index